THE NON-ELECTRIC LIGHTING SERIES

BOOK 5: Coleman Gas Lanterns

Ron Brown

Newark Valley, New York

Text and photographs by Ronald B. Brown.
Cover by FK.

Notice: This manual is designed to provide information on Coleman pressure-type lamps and lanterns.

It is not the purpose of this guide to reprint all the information that is otherwise available, but to complement, amplify, and supplement other texts and resources. You are urged to read all the available material and learn as much as you can about pressure lanterns and to tailor the information to your specific circumstances.

Every effort has been made to make this guide as complete and accurate as possible. However, there may be mistakes, both typographical and in content. Therefore this text should be used only as a general guide and not as the ultimate source of pressure lantern information. Furthermore, this guide contains information that is current only up to the printing date.

The purpose of this manual is to educate and entertain. The views, opinions, positions, and strategies expressed by the author are his alone. The author makes no representations as to the accuracy, completeness, correctness, suitability, or validity of any information in this book and will not be liable for any errors, omissions, or delays in this information or any losses, injuries, or damages arising from its use.

ISBN 978-0-9905564-6-6

Published by
R&C Publishing
15 Dr. Knapp Road South
Newark Valley, NY 13811

Printed in the United States of America

THE NON-ELECTRIC LIGHTING SERIES
BOOK 5: Coleman Gas Lanterns

Table of Contents

Foreword

Sometimes I think Coleman screwed up. They were still a new company when, in World War One, they introduced a line of pressure lanterns. Coleman produced a quality product and expanded like gangbusters for the next twenty years, bringing light to farms and ranches and remote countryside not served by the electric utilities available in the cities.

Then, in 1935, FDR signed the Rural Electrification Act and Coleman had to find other markets. Which they did. Campers and outdoorsmen. And that market lasted an additional fifty years.

But all good things must come to an end. Coleman liquid-fuel lanterns met their match with both propane lanterns and LED lanterns. With propane lanterns there's no messy spillage of liquid fuel. And battery-powered LED lanterns remove all fire hazard, allowing you to bring the light (safely) inside the tent.

The Coleman Company should have pursued a new market but didn't. And what market is that, you ask? Survivalists and preppers, I answer.

I really wish, as a prepper, I could buy a set of three new Colemans. All the same size so that as many parts as possible were interchangeable. One lantern would burn Coleman fuel and gasoline. Another would burn kerosene and diesel fuel. And a third would burn alcohol (methanol, denatured, isopropyl). There's no question but what the technology exists.

During World War Two, in Europe, there were lots of restrictions on petroleum products. So farmers made what was basically moonshine and burned it in pressure lanterns.

Those lanterns are all collector's items today. But it's known technology. It would not take a huge R&D budget to recreate those alcohol-burning lamps in the present day.

It looks to me like the Coleman Company doesn't realize that preppers even exist. But if they ever do discover us and start marketing a Survivalist Set of three lanterns, don't you think I should get a cut for providing the idea? Would that be too much to ask? Oh well. Dream on.

In the meantime, Ron Brown is continuing his lighting series. This volume deals with Coleman gas lanterns. The next will discuss pressure lanterns that burn kerosene (Petromax as well as Coleman). And, later on, a third book will address pressure lanterns that burn alcohol. (I was surprised to learn that there are actually a couple of mantle-lanterns on the market right now, available brand new, that will run on alcohol.) So we have a lot to look forward to.

I hope you're as enlightened as I am (no pun intended) by Ron's *Non-Electric Lighting Series*. I find it comforting to know that there are so many different ways to produce light. And as we move into the realm of pressure lanterns, we're not talking about twinkling candles and ambiance. We're talking about serious LIGHT. Enjoy.

Gaye Levy
April 2015

*****

Want to learn more about basic preparedness? Please visit Gaye's website at www.backdoorsurvival.com where you will find tools for creating a self-reliant lifestyle through thoughtful prepping and optimism.

"Let there be light" – *Genesis 1:3*

Introduction

W.C. Coleman started selling portable table lamps (pressurized mantle lamps) in 1909. Ten years later Coleman introduced the Quick-Lite – simplicity itself with virtually no moving parts. Even today, Quick-Lites are not truly rare. Coleman made and sold about five million of them.

Eventually, Coleman stopped making table lamps although Leacock-Coleman of Ronks, Pennsylvania still makes lamps that follow the old Quick-Lite design. It's the Leacock Model 107 that is pictured above. It's shown here with a Rayo shade though any 10" diameter shade will fit. It needn't be Coleman brand.

Point is, you can still buy a brand new Quick-Lite if desired. Almost. Today's fuel tank is stainless steel and today's generator is the same as is used on the newer Coleman 220 Instant-Lite lanterns. The lantern shown below is an Instant-Lite. One goal of this book is to explain the difference between Quick-Lites and Instant-Lites.

And as far as Leacock and Coleman are concerned, it's not altogether clear what their relationship is. According to one Web page, "Leacock-Coleman is a separate but connected company to Coleman in Wichita . . ." (www.millioncandlepower.info/otherlamp.html)

Why the fixation with Coleman?

There've been many lantern companies over the years but *The Non-Electric Lighting Series* has page after page and even entire books (like this one) devoted to Coleman. Why?

Fair question. WesternField and/or Hawthorne lanterns were sold by Montgomery Ward; some were made by the Rinnai Corporation of Japan and some by AGM (American Gas and Machine Co.).

J.C. Higgins and Ted Williams lanterns were sold by Sears; they, too, were made by AGM.

KampLite lanterns were made by the Queen Products Division of King-Seely Corp. of Albert Lea, Minnesota. Thermos lanterns were made by the Thermos Division of the King-Seely Thermos company at their Macomb, Illinois plant. King-Seely also made lanterns for Wards and Sears.

In one case the exact same lantern was badged as Blue Grass (Thermos), WesternField (Wards), and J.C. Higgins (Sears). *The same lantern.*
(Ref. http://tgmarsh.faculty.noctrl.edu/lantern/agmlantlater.html)

Every single year, the Akron Lamp and Mfg. Company of Akron, Ohio sold hundreds of thousands of pressure lanterns under its Diamond brand name . . . as well as lanterns branded for Wards and Sears.

A hundred pages of such tangled stuff would be easy to fill.

Today, from the Web site of The International Guild of Lamp Researchers (I'm paraphrasing):

- Where can I get parts for a Montgomery Ward mantle lamp (question 337)?
- . . . a Cornelius and Baker gas lamp (question 900)?
- . . . a Kamplite (questions 993 and 1311)?
- . . . an AGM lamp (questions 171 and 1100)?
- . . . a Thermos lantern (questions 1502 and 2835)?
- . . . a lamp from the Akron Lamp Co. (question 108)?
- . . . a Diamond lantern (question 496)?
- . . . a Blanchard lamp (question 5731)?
- Etcetera.

Short answer to all: **You can't.** The threads on the part you need are different. The length of part you need is different. The curvature of the part you need is different. And the part you need hasn't been made since before you were born. You may have a great lantern but it's an orphan. When it breaks, as all mechanical things do, it cannot be fixed. That makes it a bad investment for the survivalist.

Next, browse Coleman parts which is the authorized factory outlet (www.coleman.com/coleman/parts/parts_lantern.asp) and then check out the monster page at Old Coleman Parts (www.oldcolemanparts.com/). It might cost some money, but just about any lamp or lantern Coleman ever made can be put back in running condition.

Now ask me again. *Why the fixation with Coleman?*

Quick-Lite

Quick-Lites were 'match-lit.' Earlier models had been 'torch-lit.' After1930, Instant-Lite held sway. And in the 1970's, Coleman phased in 'adjustable brightness' lanterns.

We need to understand how are these critters different, one from the other. Let's start with Quick-Lite. And within Quick-Lite, let's start with generators.

Generators

In the context of lanterns, the term 'generator' confuses people. I know it did me for a long time. Having been raised in the age of electricity, when someone says 'generator,' the first thing that jumps to mind is a complex mass of windings, brushes, and capacitors.

So let's demystify. To do so, we must return to eighth-grade science. We need three things for a fire: (1) fuel, (2) oxygen, and (3) kindling temperature.

Before fuel will combine with oxygen and ignite, it must be in a gaseous state. Fuel in a liquid state will not ignite. The liquid fuel must be converted to a gas so that it can mix with gaseous oxygen. And, in the lantern world, that's the purpose of the generator. To take liquid fuel and convert it to gaseous fuel. To 'generate' a gas from a liquid.

A steam jenny (in the steam-engine world) performs a similar function. '*Jenny*' is slang for generator. A steam generator generated gaseous steam from liquid water. A simple teakettle is a kind of steam jenny.

And the generator for a Coleman lantern is little more than a length of brass tubing. Liquid fuel enters one end of the tube (under pressure that we pumped into the fuel tank). Heat is applied to the outside of the tube. The liquid inside the tube boils and turns to a gas. Gaseous fumes exit the other end of the tube. *Gas* (in the 'solid-liquid-gas' sense of things) has been *generated* from a liquid.

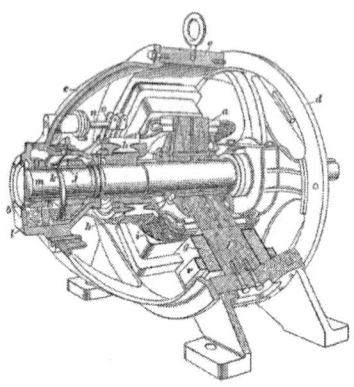

■ **ABOVE:** *An electrical generator, cutaway view. "D.-C. Motors and Generators" by Scott Hancock, 1941, page 36* ■

■ **ABOVE:** *An early Coleman generator, the Q77.* ■

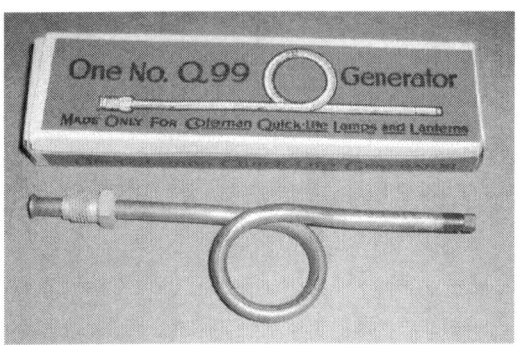

■ **ABOVE:** *Q77's were superseded by Q99's. The Q99 provides more surface area of brass and you can get the generation process started with just a couple of matches. I've seen brand new Q99's*

that were simply hollow tubes with no filler material of any kind inside. I've seen others with asbestos 'rope' inside. ■

Generators metamorphosed over the years. Early lanterns running on white gas sometimes had no **filler** material in their generators at all (Q99) but kerosene lanterns did (T44K). Today, it's reversed. Post-WWII lantern generators for gas all have filler material inside but kero lanterns do not.

Tips do get plugged. Newer generators had a 'pricker'; a needle connected to the end of a 'cleaning rod' that, with the turn of a lever, could be run back and forth through the lamp's tip while the lamp was operating. The old Q99 didn't lend itself to a cleaning rod sliding around inside because of the loop in the tube.

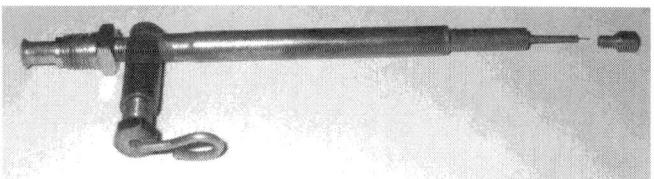

■ **ABOVE:** *An R55 generator. All Quick-Lite table lamps and lanterns will accept a Q77, Q99, or R55 generator. AND an R55 + preheat cup + Silk-Lite mantle will burn kerosene.* ■

■ **ABOVE:** *The R55's built-in cleaning rod/pricker to clear the tip was a plus. But it introduced some moving parts . . . a new level of complexity . . . a minus. To slide the pricker back-and-forth through the tip, you turned the looped cleaning lever in a circle.* ■

7

Mantles

With all the lighting devices discussed so far in *The Non-Electric Lighting Series* (candles, olive oil lamps, and kerosene wick-type lamps), the light by which we see is produced by a flame. Mantle lamps are different. With a mantle lamp, the heat from a flame causes a mantle to glow and it's the glowing mantle that is the primary source of light, not the flame.

It is planned that, later on, *The Non-Electric Lighting Series* will have an entire book devoted to mantles; even how to make them. For the moment, we only need to understand some of the basics as they apply to Coleman gas pressure lamps.

Just as a tungsten filament in an electric bulb 'incandesces' or glows from the heat of the electric current passing through the wire, so a mantle in a non-electric lamp incandesces from the heat of a flame. The light produced by the mantle is many times brighter than the light from the flame itself.

A 1922 Coleman ad said their mantles were made from "long-fibre Egyptian cotton." Rayon has also been used.

The coarsely woven mantle is soaked in a rare-earth solution, then coated with lacquer. It's the rare earth that glows in the heat of the flame and produces light. The cloth is only a carrier. Before using the mantle the first time, we burn away the lacquer and cloth. The ash skeleton left behind is what incandesces and generates light.

Throughout most of the 1900's, thorium was the rare earth used in mantles. Thorium, however, is slightly radioactive (making it a hot-button issue). In the politically-correct

1980's, thorium mantles were largely (not totally) replaced with yttrium, a rare earth that is not radioactive.

Please know that old-time thorium mantles do burn brighter and hotter than the newer yttrium mantles. And old-time Coleman-brand thorium mantles are still available on eBay. Thorium mantles are not illegal to buy, sell, make, or use.

Other brands of mantles exist (Coghlans, Stansport), and you can find them on-line, but, as far as I know, they are all yttrium. Some Peerless-brand mantles (of new manufacture and made in the Philippines) are thorium.

■ **ABOVE:** *All the Coleman mantles branded 'Silk-Lite' were thorium. Pictured here is a No. 21A Silk-Lite that would have been used on a Quick-Lite table lamp.* ■

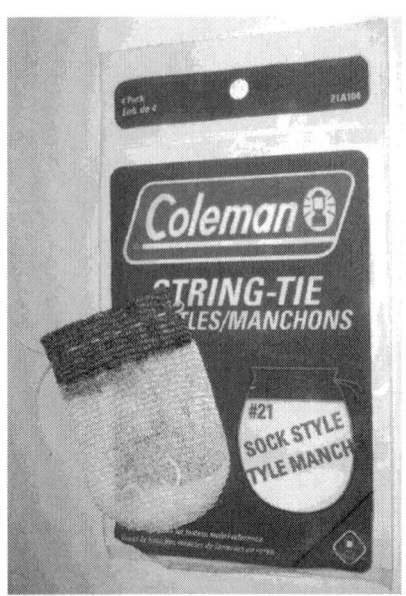

■ **ABOVE:** *The yttrium #21 (what Walmart sells today) replaced the thorium No. 21A. Both work fine on a Quick-Lite.* ■

■ **ABOVE:** *Another view of #21's. They work on (1) the old Quick-Lites and (2) the newer Instant-Lites as well as (3) the newest Dual Fuel Colemans. They are 'sock style' mantles, flexible before they are fired. They resemble miniature drawstring bags. There is only one opening, at the top, that fits over the end of the burner tube. They are hand-tied in place. Sometimes the factory-installed drawstring breaks. In that case, you can replace the drawstring with a piece of fine wire. Once fired, the mantle is rigid and pretty well stays in place all by itself.* ■

Firing

New mantles must be 'fired' before they will produce light. The factory-applied lacquer must be burned off. All that remains after firing is the ash of the cloth carrier and the rare earth. As you can imagine, mantles are rather delicate creatures.

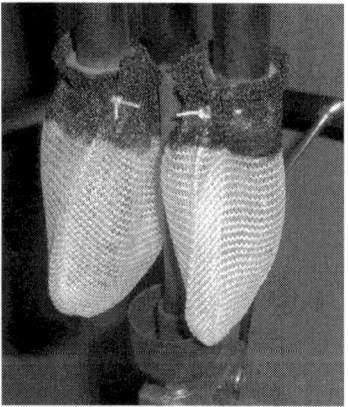

■ **ABOVE:** *New mantles, mounted, ready to be fired.* ■

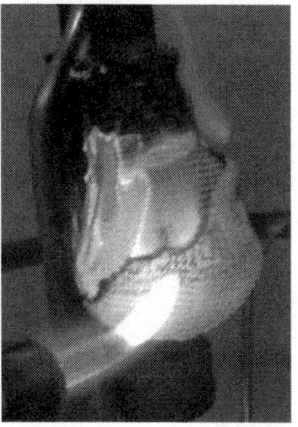

■ **ABOVE:** *A mantle being fired. You can see the flame from my torch. Matches work, too. Best do this outdoors and not inhale the smoke, especially with the older radioactive mantles.* ■

11

■ **ABOVE:** *Newly fired mantles are flaccid and limpy.* ■

■ **ABOVE:** *When you first turn on the pressurized fuel and light the newly-burned-off mantle, it puffs up like a tiny balloon and becomes rigid, holding its shape thereafter.* ■

General Operation

■ **ABOVE:** *An antique Quick-Lite in operation, here producing light equivalent to a 250-watt bulb. This is a table lamp, designed for inside use, shown here without a shade. The fuel tank is at the bottom. Gasoline flows upwards from the tank to the burners above it.* ■

■ **ABOVE:** *For the fuel to flow uphill it needs to be under pressure. Pressure is supplied by a small hand pump (lower left) resembling a bicycle tire pump. You must add a few strokes every few hours to maintain pressure. The fitting to receive the pump can be seen at 10:00 o'clock on the fuel tank. Further up the lamp, I've shown one 'arm' fitted with a mantle and one arm without so you can see where mantles are located in relation to the fuel tank and generator.* ■

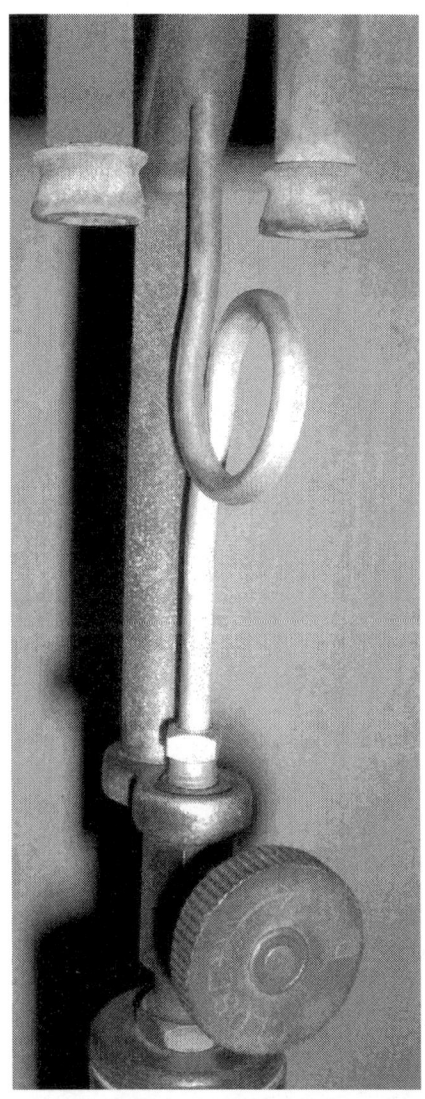

■ **ABOVE:** *Going from bottom to top, the first feature of interest above the tank is the fuel shutoff valve. Immediately above the shutoff valve is the generator, the part with the loop. Fuel flows from the tank, through the fuel valve, and into the generator. At the top end of the generator (inside the air tube where you can't see it) is a tip with a tiny hole in it.* ■

15

Tips & Stuff

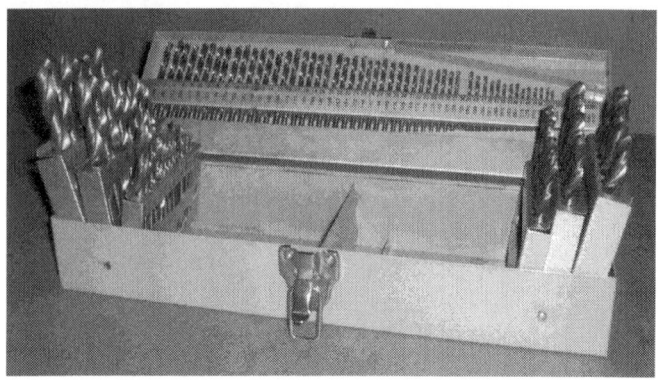

■ **ABOVE:** *A set of ordinary jobber drills. The smallest drill in the box is a #60 (that translates to .040" or $^{40}/_{1000}$ of an inch in diameter).* ■

■ **ABOVE:** *The black circle (upper right) is the bottom of a #60 drill. For comparison, the white dot in the center of the black square is the port or hole in the tip through which gaseous fuel exits a lantern generator. It is .008" or $^{8}/_{1000}$ of an inch in diameter.* ■

So riddle me this. Just HOW, a hundred years ago, before World War One, did they drill a hole $^8/_{1000}$ of an inch in diameter? To be honest, I pondered that for quite a long time.

In answer, visualize a solid block of brass into which we've drilled a one-inch hole. Now picture that block trapped between two humongous vise-grip wrenches. The north end of the hole is pulled to the north. The south end of the hole is pulled to the south. But no matter how far we pull, the hole itself, though it shrinks and shrinks, never closes up entirely. And let's say, for the sake of argument, we stop pulling when the hole gets down to .008" in diameter. And that, Johnny, is where tips come from.

■ **ABOVE:** *The top of the generator, the part with the tip, protrudes into the air tube. If the tip gets plugged, you must grab your wrench and dismount the generator from the lamp in order to clean it.* ■

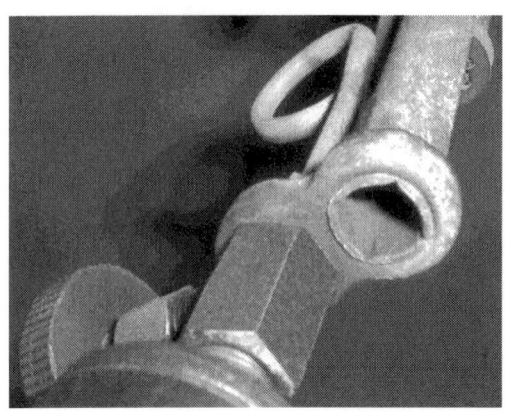

■ **ABOVE:** *Here we've positioned ourselves lower than the lamp and are looking up at it from underneath. Located near the shutoff valve is the bottom end of the air tube. It is wide open, sucking in air.* ■

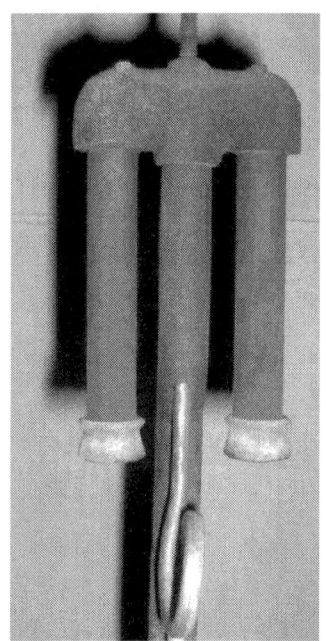

■ **ABOVE:** *The 'shoulders' at the top of the air tube constitute a mixing chamber. The gas/air mix, under pressure, travels down the 'arms' (burner tubes) to the burner nozzles.* ■

18

No provision was made in the Q99 generators to clear the hole in the tip should it become plugged. The impurities in white gas were nil. I've read that 500 to 800 hours of running time could be expected on a Q99 generator before replacement was necessary.

Torch-Lit

Before Quick-Lite, lamps had been 'torch-lit.' Actually, 'torch-preheated' would be a more accurate name.

And in the case of Quick-Lite, 'match-preheated' would be a more descriptive term than match-lit. The Q99 generator only required a couple of matches to get started.

Earlier lanterns required a *torch* to get started. But it was not a torch in the style of a modern propane soldering torch. It was more along the lines of a miniature caveman torch.

It looked like a tiny vegetable brush with asbestos bristles. The bristles were dipped in alcohol, lit, and held next to the generator for preheating. A modern-day replacement (so I'm told) can be fashioned from a fiberglass tiki-torch wick and a length of twisted wire.

■ **ABOVE:** *Before Quick-Lite, torches were used. This is a torch.* http://tgmarsh.faculty.noctrl.edu/lantern/coleuslampbeforemid192 0s.htm ■

The Quick-Lite, using matches instead of a torch, was considered a big improvement in lantern design. But after reading the directions, I sometimes shake my head in disbelief. Here are the original "**DIRECTIONS** For Assembling and Operating the Coleman Quick-Lite Lamp" that came with the lamp.

"**To Light Lamp:**

"10. Always use two matches in left hand. Apply flame to lower part of generator coil Q99. Don't open valve until matches are burned down nearly to fingers. Then open and close valve quickly with right hand. [Please keep in mind, dear reader, that you are reaching in through the little gate or door in the mica globe, pictured below, to do this.]

"11. Remove left hand with burnt ends of matches but keep right hand on valve stem Q56b a few seconds until the mantles begin to dim. Then with right hand open the valve one full turn for full light."

Globes

■ **ABOVE:** *Early lanterns had mica (isinglass) globes. Shown here is a replica. The vertical sliding gate is where you reached inside with two lit matches in your left hand. Yumpin' yimminy!* ■

■ **ABOVE:** *Instant-Lites came after Quick-Lites and did not need a gate in the globe for the insertion of hand-held matches. Rather, a hole in the floor of the lantern was provided for the insertion of a lit match. So gated mica globes could be replaced with non-gated Pyrex globes (borosilicate glass).* ■

Most of the Quick-Lite lanterns you see on eBay have horrible, ratty, mica globes. Interestingly, a glass globe from a newer 220 or 228 model will fit a Quick-Lite perfectly. And the 220/228 is probably the most common model that Coleman ever made. The 220 glass is $4^3/_4$" in diameter x $5^1/_4$" tall and is straight-sided, not curved.

Using a glass globe, of course, means there is no sliding gate for lighting. Lighting such a hybrid requires some disassembly of the lantern before lighting and reassembly after it's been fired up. It sounds inconvenient but, upon reflection, I realize that it's how I've come to light lanterns anyway.

After several years of standing at the workbench poking lit matches into impossible little holes, today I simply unscrew the ball nut at the top of the lantern, remove the ventilator and globe, and light the thing. Once it's going I put it back together. If you can live with that lighting technique, then glass globes can be used and many a Quick-Lite lantern brought back to life.

I've also seen cylinders of stainless steel wire mesh used in place of glass or mica globes. The metal mesh reduces light output but, in a SHTF scenario, it's a possibility to keep in mind for any lantern.

Filler Plug

■ **ABOVE:** *The Quick-Lite filler plug is a two-piece affair — the filler plug itself (left) plus a separate hollow air stem (right).* ■

■ **ABOVE:** *The filler plug, must be tightened with a wrench. Its gasket is lead, not rubber.* ■

■ **ABOVE:** *If you remove the plug and turn it over, you can see the ball-bearing check valve inside. Some check valves are spring-loaded. Not this one. If you shake the plug you can hear the ball rattling around in there. With the filler plug installed on the lamp and the ball in the down (open) position, air from the pump enters the tank. On the return pump stroke, the ball is sucked up and held it against the 'ceiling,' preventing the air from escaping. After half a dozen strokes, pressure alone (inside the tank) is sufficient to hold the ball against the ceiling.* ■

■ **ABOVE:** *The air stem is hollow. It screws into the center of the filler plug and provides a path for air to travel from the pump to the check valve.* ■

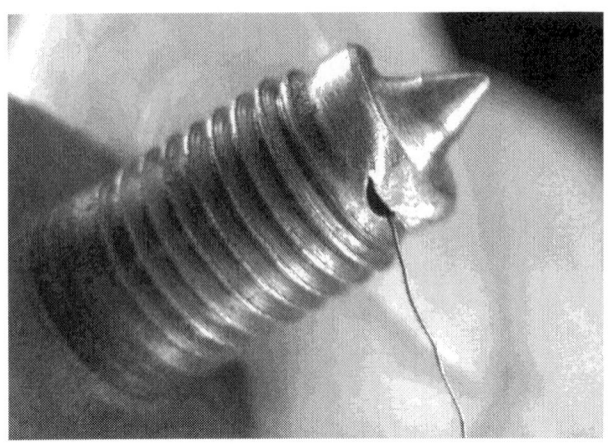

■ **ABOVE:** *So you can see/locate it, I've inserted a wire in the air stem's exit gap.* ■

■ **ABOVE:** *In use, the plug is screwed into the font and the air stem is screwed into the plug. The air stem is turned counter-clockwise to loosen and air is pumped in. Afterwards, the air stem is shut finger-tight by turning it clockwise. This provides a positive shutoff to prevent pressure from escaping regardless of anything that may happen to the ball bearing. The hollow (tiny crater) you see in the top of the air stem forms a seat for the pump.* ■

Pumps

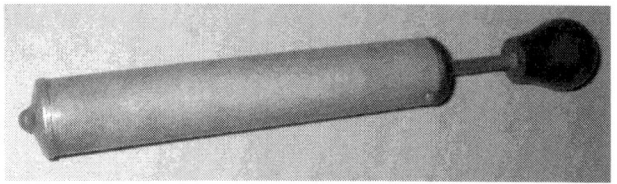

■ **ABOVE:** *Complete Quick-Lite pump.* ■

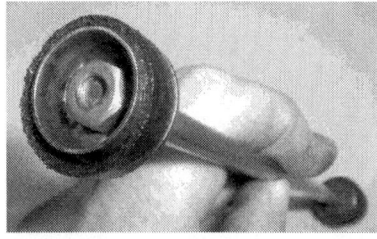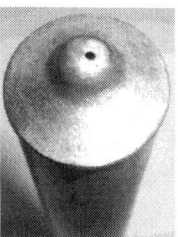

■ **ABOVE LEFT:** *Super-simple, this. Inside the brass pump tube we find a preformed pump-leather on a shaft. And that's it; nothing else.* **ABOVE RIGHT:** *This is the hole in the end of the pump where the air comes out.* ■

■ **ABOVE:** *The old Quick-Lites used external pumps. The newer Instant-Lites used built-in pumps.* ■

Despite their nickname ("gas bombs"), the early Coleman table lamps were actually very safe. Old W.C. understood that, as a business model, it was counterproductive to blow up customers and burn down their houses.

■ **ABOVE:** *An authentic Quick-Lite lantern from the 1920's with its Q99 generator and mica globe. The fundamental difference between an inside 'lamp' and an outside 'lantern' is that the lantern has a globe. The purpose of the globe is to stop bugs from flying into the mantles and committing hari-kari. Inside, no bugs equates to no need for a globe.* ■

According to Neil McRae (revered as the lantern god on various internet lamper forums), ". . . the best lanterns Coleman ever made were the 1920s Quick-Lite models. No fiddling around with fuel pick up systems and no moving parts; they just work and are near indestructible." – The International Guild of Lamp Researchers, Question 5282

From a reliability point of view, Quick-Lites are indeed bulletproof. From the survivalist's point of view, they are collector's items (and that means expensive).

What came after Quick-Lite? Instant-Lite

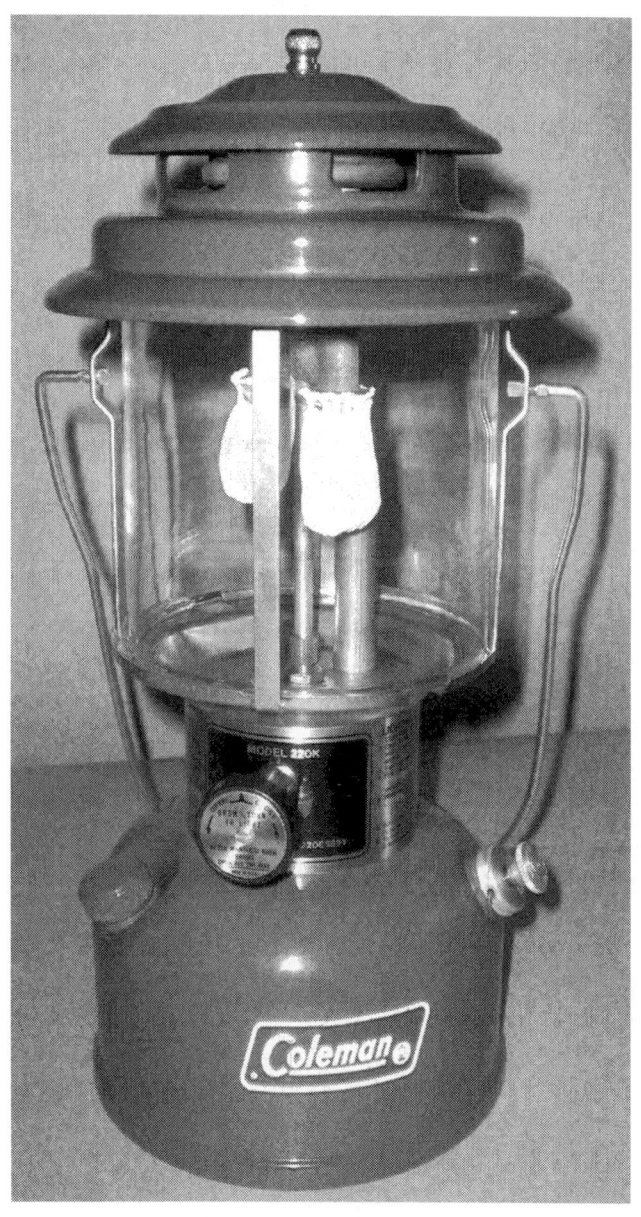

Most of what we just learned about Quick-Lites (firing the mantles, for example) is directly translatable to Instant-Lites.

The 'Instant-Lite' concept was introduced in 1929 (15 years before the Model 220 pictured above) and put Coleman far ahead of its competition. Coleman engineers had come up with a way to virtually eliminate preheating.

If you follow the directions on the Instant-Lite fuel valve (pictured a bit further on), at $^1/_4$ turn you pull some air into the mixing chamber along with the gasoline. That mixture will ignite without preheating and make the mantles incandesce.

After running in this fashion for a few minutes, the lantern becomes hot enough for fuel to vaporize in the generator and for the process to become self-sustaining. At that point, turning the fuel valve all the way OPEN shuts off the preliminary air and switches to the regular fuel pickup.

It's a clever way to get the lantern to do its own preheating. But it only works for gasoline, not kerosene. Kerosene is not volatile enough. There are no Instant-Lite kerosene lanterns.

HOW TO USE and ENJOY YOUR NEW...

Coleman

220F & 228F LANTERN

■ **ABOVE:** *The Coleman 220 had a fraternal twin, the Coleman 228. The only difference between the two was the ventilator or 'hat' size. The 228 hat was 8.5" in diameter whereas the 220 was 7". All else was the same. They even shared the same instruction manual. The 228 cost a few dollars more and so was less common. As we speak, there are 70 big-hat 228's for sale on eBay.* ■

■ **ABOVE:** *The Instant-Lite 200A was Coleman's second most popular lantern after the 220/228. Introduced in 1952, it was smaller, had one mantle, and output 200 watts-worth of light. Again, as we speak, there are 120 for sale on eBay.* ■

For the prepper, the 200A makes more sense than the 220/228. Mantles are the Achilles' heel of pressure lanterns. Mantles are fragile. They do not take well to the vibration of automobile transportation, for example. When you get down to your last couple of spare mantles, do you want, at that moment, a lantern that can run on ONE mantle? Or a lantern that demands TWO?

Side note. 'Auto transport' puts me in mind of a suggestion I once read. One way to protect an already-fired Coleman mantle (so they say) is to spray the mantle with m'lady's lacquer hair spray before transport. Upon reaching your destination, the lacquer is burned off (similar to the original firing) before the lantern is lit. It certainly sounds good though I can't vouch for it from personal experience.

Back to our story. Interestingly, the Coleman 220 outputs 250 watts-worth of light (with two mantles) whereas the Coleman 200A outputs 200 watts-worth of light, 80% as much, using one mantle. Does that make sense? Shouldn't the lantern with only one mantle output 50% as much light? How can one mantle output 80% as much as two mantles?

■ **ABOVE:** *A Coleman 200A (left) burns white gas and uses one #21 mantle. A Coleman 220 (right) burns white gas and uses two*

#21 mantles. My observation is that the 200A outputs 200 watts-worth of light and the Model 220 outputs 250 watts-worth. How can one mantle produce 80% of two mantles? ■

How can this be?

How? Because light output is a function of fuel consumption, not mantle count.

The 220 has a tip aperture of .008 inches. The 200A has a tip aperture of .007 inches. Theoretically, the light output of the 200A should be 87.5% of the 220, not 80% (.007 ÷ .008 = .875).

Why isn't it? Pressure. There's is no accurate way to measure the pressure inside the Coleman font. 'Pressure' is entirely an estimate based on the pump's resistance to one's thumb.

Are we having fun yet?

■ **ABOVE:** *An Instant-Lite fuel valve looks like this.* ■

■ **ABOVE:** *The fuel valve (black knob) is on the left; the cleaning lever on the right.* ■

■ **ABOVE:** *A close-up of the little crank (called a lever) that operates the cleaning rod. It's the cleaning rod that has the needle or pricker mounted on its end. Turning the crank round and round guides the pricker in and out of the hole in the tip.* ■

Coleman produced lots of different Instant-Lite models. One-mantle and two-mantle types. For the military. For *foreign* militaries. For the railroads. For campers. For export. With brass fonts and steel fonts. Badged for Sears and badged for Wards. They had more model numbers than the government had agencies.

Well, no. That's not possible.

What's <u>best</u> for preppers?

In my opinion, the lantern models just described (220, 228, and 200A Instant-Lites) are the prepper's best choices for burning white gas (Coleman fuel).

Coleman made a ton of them. That means they are widely available (from lawn sales, flea markets, and eBay). They are cheap; cheaper than brand new Coleman Dual Fuels. They are widely recognized and understood. And spares parts (both new and used) are readily available.

And they are reliable. No question about that. AND, if push comes to shove, these three models can be converted to burn kerosene. (Although that's another story and must wait for the next book in this series, *Book 6: Kerosene Pressure Lanterns.*)

If you already have an old Coleman, of course, no matter what the model number, and it can be put back in running condition with some elbow grease and a $10 generator, then by all means that's the route to go. You'll never get anything cheaper. But be careful. A $10 generator followed by a $10 pump followed by a $5 fill cap followed by a $15 globe is not a bargain.

If you're starting from scratch (or if you need a second lantern for camp or barn or boat), then, again, a 220 or 228 or 200A will give you the biggest bang for the buck.

FWIW, here's a tip for buying a lantern on eBay. First, find a lantern that is pictured burning. A verbal description saying it's been tested and is operational is not nearly as good as an actual photo of the lantern in operation. Second, find a seller who has a 100% approval rating. A picture of the lantern in operation AND a 100% approval rating from other customers is what you seek. The seller will do handstands to protect that precious 100% rating.

What's <u>worst</u> for preppers?

Tough question. It's difficult to be specific but there are some generalities: (1) Avoid orphans; you can't get parts. (2) Avoid collectibles; they're unnecessarily expensive. (3) Avoid old stuff that's prone to breakage. Generally speaking, 'old stuff' translates into World War Two or earlier.

The 'orphan issue' creates an immediate conflict between you, the customer, and Coleman, the producer. Coleman likes orphans. As do many other companies with many other kinds of merchandise. If they can entice you into buying an orphan, then they've created a captive customer for spare parts.

But on your side of the river, when you need a spare part (generator, mantle, glass globe), then is not the time to own an orphan. And needing that spare part will always happen at the worst possible moment . . . when the river's five feet high and risin'. . . it's a law of nature.

The Coleman NorthStar is a good example. It's Coleman's top-of-the-line Dual-Fuel lantern. It's been around since

1995. (Coleman also makes a propane NorthStar as well as an LED/battery-powered NorthStar.)

The white-gas NorthStar employs a unique, pleated, tubular mantle. Except for Coleman's propane NorthStar, none of the zillion other lanterns in the world has it or can use it – new, used, or antique. To me, it's the King of Orphans.

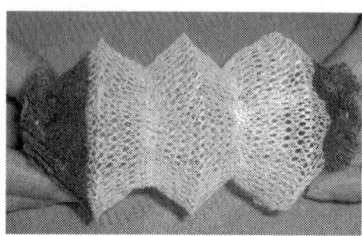

■ **ABOVE:** *A Coleman #95 mantle for the NorthStar. How many campers in the state park will have a spare to share?* ■

■ **ABOVE:** *A Coleman 236 on the left and a Coleman 242C on the right. I've turned the lanterns so that the fill caps are close to each other for size comparison. The 242C is an early Instant-Lite with the directions on the collar, not the knob.* ■

The larger of the two lanterns pictured above, the Coleman 236, was intended as a white-gas sister to the Coleman 237 kerosene lantern. Both the 236 and 237 were big 500 candlepower lanterns. The 237 is touted by many enthusiasts as the best kerosene lantern of all time. But its white-gas 236 sibling was never very popular and, as a result, is today rare. And that means expensive. And if you think the 236 lantern is rare, the 236 generator is super-rare. This is a collector's item, not a good choice for day-to-day lighting and day-to-day survival. And so we can elucidate our second GFP (Generalization For Preppers): stay away from collector's items.

Aside. If you have sharp eyes, you'll note that the 236 pictured above has a preheat cup mounted on the generator (even though, as an Instant-Lite intended for Coleman fuel, a preheat cup is completely unnecessary). To tell the truth, I'd been experimenting, attempting to burn kerosene in the 236, and forgot to remove the preheat cup before I snapped the picture.

The smaller 242C has its own problems. It falls into the 'old stuff' category. For one thing, the fill cap on the fuel tank is smaller than what is used today. From the first model 220C Instant-Lite in 1944 right through today's Dual Fuel lanterns, Coleman has used the same size filler cap on all its fuel tanks. But the 242C is smaller, older, obsolete. And fill caps do give trouble. It seems like a trivial issue – until it's you who needs the light and it's your lantern that won't hold pressure.

And so we have our third Generalization For Preppers: stay away from older, obsolete, non-standard models. The 242C ventilator, below, drives the point home.

■ **ABOVE:** *A 242C ventilator. The spot welding failed. I've never seen this before. Why me, Lord?* ■

Repairs

• Instant-Lites were produced through the 1980's. They are arguably the best lanterns ever made . . . with one caveat. After standing for a long time (read *years*), the fuel/air valve (down inside the lantern) can stick and all you get is air. The fuel-feed needle-valve does not retract and let in fuel from the bottom. If you shake the lantern, the air intake at the top of the fuel-feed tube receives a little splashed-in gas so the lamp will run for a few seconds and then die.

If you try and remove the fuel/air tube from the font, please know that it was put in TIGHTLY. It was not made to be removable. Rather, it was made to never, ever, ever leak.

• Fill caps can give problems (because the gasket material wears out and the lamp will not hold pressure). You can add an O-ring as a supplemental gasket but that takes up space and means very few cap-threads will remain to engage font-threads. Whatever threads do exist must withstand a fair amount of stress. So it's best if you burn out the old gasket with a propane or butane torch. It will become brittle and you can chip it out of the fill cap with a small screwdriver (after it cools, please).

38

● Another common problem involves the foot-valve or check-valve at the base of the built-in pump. It can freeze up. Sometimes it can be freed up with WD-40. If not, replacing it is tricky business. You can find directions on-line, both on YouTube in addition to http://light.papo-art.com/tech-n-info/Coleman_technical/coleman_valve_removal.htm. Your odds are 50/50 for a successful repair even with special tools. Half the time you'll be able to get the old foot-valve out so as to replace it. And half the time you'll ruin the lantern.

Sometimes, a lantern that's for sale at a flea market or on eBay has already been ruined by an attempted fix of the pump's foot valve. That's why it's for sale. The seller bats her baby blues at you. Everything's just perfect, she coos, except that the pump sticks a little bit.

■ **ABOVE:** *Pictured here are some special, custom-made tools for lantern repair. You'll have to limber up your Google finger to find them but they do exist. Sometimes I think that lantern repair would be a highly barterable skill in a SHTF situation.* ■

● FWIW, here's a workaround if the pump's foot valve (on an Instant-Lite) is stuck in the closed position. Get a fill cap for a Leacock table lamp, available brand new from Leacock-Coleman in Ronks, PA (a.k.a. Peak Distribution). Install the new Leacock fill cap on the Instant-Lite (NOTE: an old

Quick-Lite plug will not fit). Ignore the Instant-Lite's built-in pump. Pressurize the Instant-Lite with an old external Quick-Lite pump. It works. Oh, what a clever fellow am I.

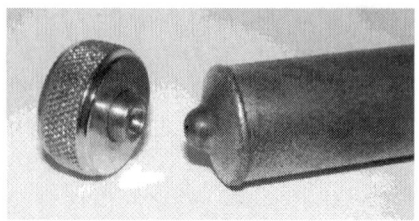

Non-Adjustable Brightness

With Instant-Lites, the instructions always said, "Do not adjust light output." In other words, the lantern was either ON or OFF with no in-between. Why? And how would you adjust light output anyway? And what would be the harm?

There are three ways of adjusting light output: (1) by the amount of pressure you pump into the lantern, (2) by adjusting the shutoff valve and restricting the amount of fuel going to the burners, and (3) by adjusting the cleaning rod with its pricker to restrict fuel flow.

I believe we need to understand the pros and cons of these options because the next step in Coleman evolution, after Instant-Lites, was 'adjustable brightness' lanterns. That's what's on the market today.

So let's explore Instant-Lites a bit further. First up, pressure. If the lantern's light is dim, you can make it brighter by pumping in more pressure. No harm in that. If your light is too intense, however, and you want to reduce it, the only way to accomplish that feat (using pressure) would be to loosen the cap on the fuel tank and let some pressure escape (like letting air out of a tire). Not the best idea in the world.

The danger lies in the fact that the escaping air is not just air. It contains vaporized fuel. You can smell it. You can see it condense on a cool surface. And it's just inches away from a glowing mantle. If the fuel you have thus vented ignites, you will get a 'flash burn' even though the lantern itself will probably not explode. (Try it and let me know, okay?)

Second, adjusting the fuel valve. It doesn't work. Not with an Instant-Lite. Technically speaking, the fuel valve is a 'needle valve' – a tapered stem, coming to a point, mating with a concave conical seat. What frustrates this as a fuel-restriction device (in an Instant-Lite) is the air-fuel mix feature. Unless the valve is wide open, you're bringing in air along with the fuel. The fuel valve simply does not work to regulate Instant-Lite brightness.

Third, adjusting the pricker. That *does* work. Light output is easily adjusted using the cleaning lever. So why not do it? Coleman never says *why*. They just say *don't*. My speculation (and it's just that, speculation) is that the generator tip is made of soft brass and the pricker will never be perfectly centered. In time, with pressurized gases streaming by, the tiny hole in the tip will wear egg-shaped and enlarge. And then the lantern will not operate properly. There may be a different reason for Coleman's decree but, if so, I don't know what it is.

for any other purpose.
7. Leave Control Knob in **OFF** position unless lantern is being lit or is in operation.
8. Do not adjust light output.
9. KEEP OUT OF THE REACH OF CHILDREN.

Adjustable Brightness & Dual Fuel

Burning Petrol

This is a good spot to recap our gasoline history lessons from *Book 3: Lantern Fuels*, an earlier book in The Non-Electric Lighting Series.

In the beginning, God created heaven (the Model 'T' Ford) and earth (Coleman table lamps). They both ran on white gas. White gas had no additives; it evaporated so cleanly it was used as dry cleaning fluid. White gas was 50 octane.

To get better performance, automobiles increased their compression ratios and 50-octane gas couldn't cut it. Engines 'knocked' on 50-octane gas. Adding tetraethyl lead was the cheapest way to increase octane.

Leaded car-gas outsold white lantern-gas at the pump so white gas became harder and harder to find. Coleman finally began selling white gas branded as 'Coleman fuel.'

Leaded automobile gas was not a good lantern fuel. In that respect it was similar to the lead-core wicks in votive candles. Inhaling lead particles floating around in the air is not good for children's brains.

The decade of the 1970's was an eco-conscious period. Lead-based house paint was out. Leaded gasoline was out. Asbestos siding shingles were out. MSDS sheets were in. Lead and asbestos both became hot-button words.

Some gas stations sold the old leaded gas. Some sold the new unleaded. Some stations had two tanks and sold both. In 1978 I bought a new Jeep Cherokee that ran on either leaded or unleaded. As such it was a novelty. Most cars required one or the other and sometimes it was hard to find the one you needed. We were in a transition period.

In 1976 Coleman brought out the Model 275. It was a transitional product. It featured adjustable brightness but, with leaded gasoline still dominating the petrol market, it was not billed as dual-fuel. Brown in color, the 275 matched the coppertone kitchen appliances of the day. Unfortunately, what the Edsel was to Ford, the brown 275 was to Coleman. It was dubbed "the Coleman turd."

The Coleman 275

■ **ABOVE:** *Coleman 275. Produced in the 1970's and 80's. White gas only. Adjustable brightness.* ■

The Web page of T.G. Marsh contains images of 275 valve assemblies taken apart and numbered, accompanied with this commentary:

> "Model 275 was the first US made Coleman lantern to use a Schrader valve for fuel control . . . Model 275A . . . only has Off and On positions and has a '. . . a very delicate balance in fume (cold starting/lighting) and liquid fuel vapourisation. This is done by means of a carefully machined orifice at the bottom of the fuel and air tube...' (Nathan Schum)." [sic]
> http://tgmarsh.faculty.noctrl.edu/lantern/coleuslant6180.htm

A Schrader valve? That sounds very scientific. Turns out a Schrader valve is merely the stem core of a bicycle inner tube; a spring-loaded check valve.

The 275's on/off knob controlled two things simultaneously: [1] the Schrader valve (controlling the flow of liquid fuel out of the font and into the generator) and [2] the pricker (controlling the flow of fuel, now a gas, out of the generator).

The 275 gained a reputation for occasionally turning into a fireball. The on-line collectors' forums placed the blame on the failure of the rubber used in the Schrader valves. I'm not so sure.

I don't know what kind of rubber it was that Coleman used in their Schrader valves – nitrile rubber or Butyl or neoprene or something else. But automobile fuel lines were made from nitrile rubber in that era and they did disintegrate over the years. And the rubber gasket in a lantern's filler cap . . . it, too, fails with time and chemical attack. But brand new? Not after thirty years. *Brand new?* Hard to believe that the fireball issue was due to the failure of Schrader-valve rubber in a new lantern.

44

Today, collectors think they're safe if they get a Schrader valve made with Viton, a brand of fluoropolymer elastomer synthetic rubber that's highly resistant to chemical attack (though *where* you get one, exactly, is a well-guarded secret). They may be deluding themselves. Even Viton has a shelf life; rubber deteriorates with time.

■ **ABOVE:** *The valve assembly from a 275. The fuel/air tube (that extends down into the font) is at the bottom. The tiny hole into which you hook the bottom of the cleaning rod/pricker can be seen at the top.* ■

■ **ABOVE:** *The fuel/air tube has been unscrewed from the assembly. The top of the Schrader valve can be seen poking its nose out of the tube.* ■

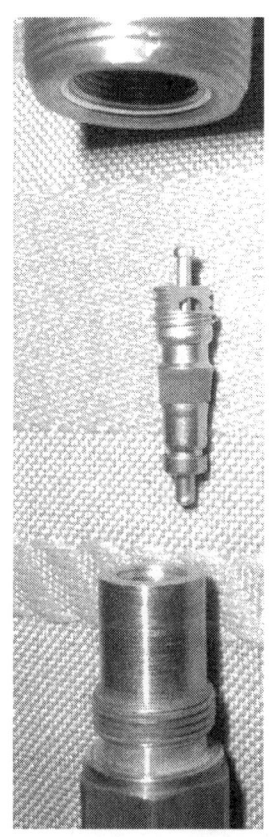

■ **ABOVE:** *The Schrader valve unscrewed from the fuel/air tube. The collectors' forums warn against replacing a lantern Schrader valve with a tire-tube Schrader valve. The rubber will not stand up to chemical attack. If you're searching for a replacement valve, Schrader valves with more exotic rubber are used in air conditioning and automobile fuel injectors.* ■

Note we're going one step at a time. With **Instant-Lite** you could burn only white gas and you could not adjust the brightness. With the **275** you could adjust the brightness but could still burn only white gas. With the newer **Dual-Fuel** (yet to be discussed), auto gas can be burned in addition to white gas AND brightness can be adjusted as well.

47

Here's something to noodle on. *Reliability*, in engineering terminology, is defined as "the probability that a device will perform its required function under stated conditions for a specific period of time."

Well, the "specific period of time" for <u>rubber</u> cannot be *forever*. Or even a hundred years. Sooner or later, every Schrader valve will fail. That's a given.

The Dual Fuel

■ **ABOVE:** *The Dual Fuel; from the 1980's to date. It burns either white gas or automobile gas. It has adjustable brightness.* ■

By the 1980's, leaded automobile gas was largely gone from the market and Coleman could introduce the Dual Fuel lineup – the 285, the Powerhouse, the NorthStar. They were all adjustable brightness *and* dual fuel. The two fuels in question were white gas and automobile gas. Lead was no longer a problem. Impurities might be a problem but not lead.

How did the Dual Fuel lanterns perform on automobile gas? Not everyone was a fan:

> "Bought this lantern when they first came out with the dual fuel concept from Coleman. Works fine as long as you feed it only white gas and nothing else. Avoid gasoline like the plague because you will only get one time use and after that next refill it will not work. The . . . gasoline . . . will clog up the generator and make the lantern useless."
> www.trailspace.com/gear/coleman/2-mantle-dual-fuel-lantern/review/20000/

It was a common complaint. But fair? Don't know. Sounds like testing time.

• First of all, I discovered the Dual Fuel 285 gave less light on automobile gas than on white gas. On white gas, it produced light equivalent to a 150-watt electric bulb. On automobile gas, 100-watts.

• Day 1. I filled the 285 with petrol (automobile gas). It started out operating at 100 watts. I kept it pumped up hard. Eight hours later, it had faded to 40 watts. At nine hours I shut it down, almost empty, running under 25 watts.

• Day 2. I filled the 285 with petrol. It started out at 100 watts. Six hours later it had faded to 40 watts. At nine hours I shut it down, running under 25 watts.

- Day 3. I filled the 285 with petrol. It started out at 100 watts. Three hours later it had faded to 40 watts. At nine hours I shut it down, running under 25 watts.

- Day 4. I filled the 285 with petrol. It started out at 40 watts. At nine hours I shut it down, running under 25 watts.

- Day 5. I switched back to white gas. Light output was 75 watts, *half* of what it had been prior to running automobile gas. It was obvious to me that auto gas had clogged the filler material (a cardboard cylinder) inside the generator.

On white gas, 36 hours of operation would have cost $4. On petrol, 36 hours of operation cost $1 in gas plus $12 for a new generator.

Looked at another way, the lantern operated above 40 watts for a total of seventeen hours before the generator was effectively plugged.

How about the old-time Instant-Lites? They were manufactured back in the days of white gas and leaded automobile gas. You wouldn't *want* to have burned automobile gas in those days because of the lead. But how about today with unleaded? Can you run today's automobile gas in the old Instant-Lites?

From a lantern-safety point of view, the answer is yes. You can run automobile gas in an Instant-Lite. The risk is not one of explosion or fire hazard. The risk is that of fouling the generator. In fact, I found the old Instant-Lites run *longer* on automobile gas than do the new, so-called Dual Fuels. My old Coleman 220 ran over 40 hours at 250-watt equivalency on automobile gas with no fading at all.

Granted, the generator/filler was a gooey mess afterwards. I thought if I stopped using it that it would harden and I would have to change the generator. I was surprised to go back weeks later and have the lantern start with no problem and run at 250-watts. Neither one is perfect, but in my opinion the old Instant-Lites are better 'dual fuel' lanterns than the new so-called Dual Fuels.

Caution – Automobile Gas (Petrol)

I experimented at some length with petrol, trying to identify which lamps would run on it, how long before the generator became fouled, etc. But over time I become convinced that burning petrol inside your living quarters is not a good thing.

Running unleaded petrol in a Quick-Lite table lamp, for example, results in a gritty substance building up on the glass globe. No other fuel does that. It feels like sandpaper; it requires Scotch-Brite to remove.

White gas is 50 octane; petrol is 87 octane. Whatever ingredients are used to raise the octane level, for sure some byproducts of combustion remain in the air for you to breathe after the gasoline proper has been consumed. Burned MTBE (methyl tertiary butyl ether) does not a good substitute for oxygen make.

Can you burn petrol in a table lamp and get away with it? Of course. Can you raise your kids on beer instead of milk and get away with it? Sure. They'll live. Kids are tough.

To be clear on this, I personally recommend against using automobile gas in any lamp or lantern. The fact that the lantern will successfully burn the stuff is not the issue. Are the byproducts of combustion safe to breathe? THAT is the question.

51

Adjustable Brightness

■ **ABOVE:** *An old-generation Coleman Instant-Lite fuel valve. The owners' manuals always said, "Never adjust light output."* ■

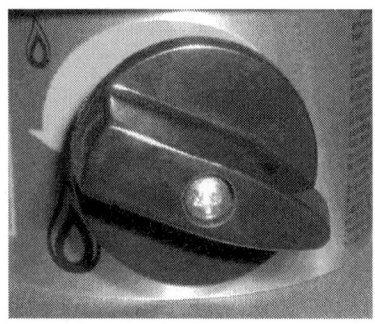

■ **ABOVE:** *Coleman adjustable-brightness fuel valve on today's lanterns. The instructions say, "Adjust fuel valve to desired brightness . . . Part of the brightness control is located in the generator."* ■

The adjustable brightness feature concerned me. With only one knob, it appeared to me that Coleman was making the pricker do triple duty: (1) cleaning the tip when it got plugged, (2) acting as a shutoff valve, and (3) adjusting brightness. But why would that be considered safe today? It never used to be.

My fears came from reading about kerosene pressure lanterns. Petromax, for example, has a spring-loaded check valve or foot valve in the font that works in tandem with the pricker in the generator. Turning the control knob one way opens the foot valve and simultaneously opens the pricker. Liquid fuel is allowed from the font to the generator; gaseous fuel is simultaneously allowed from the generator to the mantle.

But there are a few lanterns (all kerosene) – Optimus, Vapalux, Col-Max 555, and some Bialaddin models – that, according to my reading (or according to my understanding of my reading), rely entirely on the pricker to control everything. Good heavens! Is that what Coleman is doing with a *gas* lantern?

And Coleman's statement that "part of the brightness control is located in the generator" further mystified me. What could that part be other than the pricker?

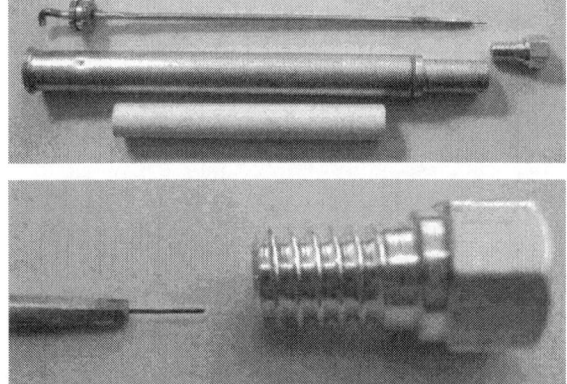

■ **ABOVE:** *I had an extra Dual Fuel generator on hand so I took it apart. The white cardboard tube "is used for heat transfer and to slow the flow of fuel" according to oldcolemanparts.com. But there is no spring, interestingly enough, as there is in an Instant-Lite generator. The pricker was the only part I could identify that had the ability to adjust fuel flow. (See the little dimple in the left end of the barrel. These generators are 'crimped' and you are not supposed to take them apart. Spoils the mystique, I suppose.)* ■

I finally decided to take a whole lantern apart – a brand new 285 Dual Fuel – and see what made it tick (hoping all the while I'd be clever enough to get it back together again). I satisfied myself that it's not just the pricker shutting off fuel; the single control knob simultaneously regulates [1] the liquid fuel flowing from the font to the generator as well as [2] the gaseous fuel (via the pricker) flowing from the generator to the mantles. (And, yes, I did get it back together . . . after some help from all the king's horses.)

Even so, the new Dual Fuel, adjustable-brightness lanterns are a far cry from the Quick-Lites of yore that boasted virtually no moving parts. On June 25, 2011, a contributor to The Coleman Collectors Forum said:

> "I took the coleman facory training . . . anytime any of the newer gas lanterns came in they had a big rolling bin that they chunked them in and at the end of the work day it was my job to roll it over to the compactor and mash them . . . they said it was more cost effective to just replace them [instead of repairing them]. They took great care in the repairs of the older lanterns becuase they knew that many poeple had a sentimental attachment . . ." [sic]
> http://colemancollectorsforum.websitetoolbox.com/post?id=5367248&goto=nextoldest

Safety
Coleman Fuel

Perhaps the greatest single danger with Coleman pressure lanterns is the handling and storage of Coleman fuel (white gas) outside the lantern. The lantern itself is a sealed, closed-loop system. Once inside the lantern, Coleman fuel is quite safe. The bigger danger lies with the gas can kicking around in the back of your pickup.

And refilling a white-gas lantern by the light of another lantern, or by the light of a campfire (read live flame) . . . now *that's* walking with the angels . . .

Mantles & Globes

Mantles are delicate. Holes can easily develop and are fairly dangerous. Lanterns get jiggled and jostled a lot. If a hole does occur, you can see a spike or ray of flame exiting the hole. If that ray touches the glass globe and rests there for any length of time it will etch the glass. The picture below shows a globe that has been etched in just this fashion.

I was curious as to how hot a flame it takes to etch a Pyrex globe. So I lit a propane soldering torch and held it on one spot for five minutes. It did not etch the glass. It did, however, soften the glass and make it sag in that spot.

■ **ABOVE:** *Etched from a flawed mantle.* ■

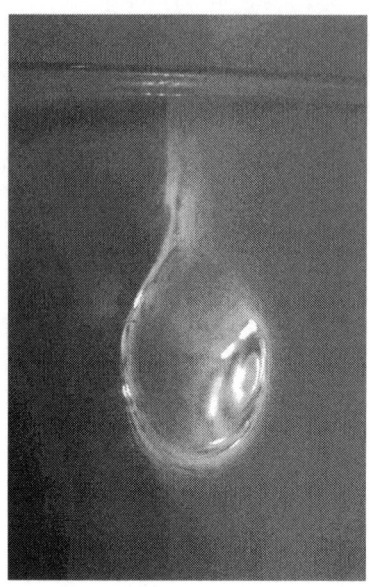

■ **ABOVE:** *Softened from a propane torch.* ■

Now . . . if a hole appeared in the *bottom* of a mantle and the spike of flame was aimed downwards at the floor of the burner cage . . . could it chew a hole through the floor of the cage as well as the top of the fuel tank? I will leave that experiment in your capable hands, thank you very much.

Indoor Use

Is it safe to use a gasoline pressure lantern indoors?

My 1920 Quick-Lite table lamp runs on white gas and uses two #21 mantles. It was sold for inside use.

My 1964 Instant-Lite lantern (model 220F) runs on white gas and uses two #21 mantles. Its instructions are silent on the topic of inside use.

56

My 1983 Instant-Lite lantern (model 220K) runs on white gas and uses two #21 mantles. Its instructions say: "This lantern consumes air (oxygen). Do not use in unventilated areas. Ample ventilation must be provided. Provide additional ventilation for persons and other fuel burning appliances occupying the same enclosed area."

My 2010 adjustable-brightness Dual Fuel lantern runs on white gas and uses two #21 mantles. Its instructions say: "Always light and use lantern outdoors; never inside house."

So what changed? The fuel? The oxygen? The laws of physics? The science of litigation?

There are legitimate concerns. Namely, oxygen starvation and carbon monoxide.

Oxygen Starvation

Outside air is 21% oxygen. Inside air is something below that. You, your wood stove, your birthday candles, your girlfriend, and the family dog all compete for the available oxygen. If the oxygen level is depleted too far you suffer 'oxygen starvation.'

You say you feel 'just fine' even though you are pale and confused. Later, you have no energy/strength/stamina. You have shortness of breath, chest tightness, blue coloring around your lips, tingling fingers, increased pulse, you want to sleep.

The fix is easy. Ditch the girlfriend. Well, okay. Open a window. Let in some fresh air.

Your wood stove has a chimney and is thus 'vented.' Venting gets rid of unwanted products of combustion. Your gas range in the kitchen (typically four burners plus an oven) is not vented. But whether an appliance is vented or not, the oxygen it uses in the burning process comes from the inside air.

Oxygen starvation can also occur at high altitudes (where the air is 'thin') and when breathing mixtures of gases with low oxygen content (e.g. diving).

What are the long-term consequences if you ignore the symptoms of oxygen starvation?

Answer. Extreme fatigue, waking at night gasping for breath, loss of eyesight, loss of short term memory, progressive weakening of the heart muscle leading to heart failure.

But that's the long-term extreme. Again, as far as fuel-burning lamps and lanterns are concerned, the fix is easy. Open a window. Let in some fresh air.

Carbon Monoxide

Big topic, this. As a youngster, I was repeatedly lectured on the dangers of carbon monoxide. Why? Because my mother had two schoolmates die from carbon monoxide. It made quite an impression on her tiny high school graduating class of twelve students.

The victims had been out 'parking' in a Model 'A' Ford. To keep warm, they'd left the engine idling and the heater on. Heat for the Model 'A' was pulled from the exhaust manifold. It was a poor design, well known for leaking exhaust gases. In this case it proved fatal.

(You might feel better knowing that, today, a car's heater extracts heat from the hot water in the cooling system, not from the exhaust system.)

Carbon monoxide (CO is the chemical symbol) is produced when something burns with insufficient oxygen being present.

Things that smolder (cigarettes, pipes, incense, cigars, charcoal briquettes) give off carbon monoxide in considerable quantity. That's why it's not safe to use a charcoal grill inside the house. In contrast, things that burn with an open flame produce very little carbon monoxide.

The smoldering concept is simple enough to demonstrate. If you want to test your carbon monoxide detector, bring a burning stick of incense nearby. The detector will inform you of the presence of carbon monoxide in no uncertain terms.

But the smoldering concept can also be confusing. Why does something smolder and not burn? After all, it has oxygen. It has access to the same air that we're breathing.

The answer is that it doesn't have ENOUGH oxygen. Each material has its own threshold of how much oxygen is required to burn with an open flame. Firewood will burn with the amount of oxygen found in the open air. Tobacco will smolder. Steel will not even smolder.

But an oxyacetylene cutting torch doesn't MELT a hole in steel. It BURNS a hole in steel. When you squeeze the lever, pure oxygen is introduced at the welding tip and the steel literally *burns*.

Think about all the restrictions around medical patients who are on oxygen. Various materials will ignite and burn in a high-oxygen atmosphere that won't burn, or will merely smolder, in our regular atmosphere.

So let me say it again. Carbon monoxide is produced when something burns with insufficient oxygen being present. Insufficient oxygen, that is, for the material at hand, for the material that is smoldering.

There are three ways that a condition of 'insufficient oxygen' can come about.

(1) To burn with an open flame, the fuel in question (tobacco, for example) needs more oxygen than is present in ordinary air. We just covered that.

(2) The device (a stove burner, for example) can be out of adjustment; the fuel/air ratio can be incorrect. With propane, a 'lean' burn (not enough fuel) can be recognized when flames lift away from the burner and tend to go out. A 'rich' burn (too much fuel) results in large yellow flames. (Propane flames should be blue.) Both rich and lean burns reveal incomplete combustion and imply the production of carbon monoxide.

(3) In an enclosed area (room, cellar, shed, house trailer), combustion can deplete the available oxygen with the result that carbon monoxide (CO) is produced as a byproduct of combustion rather than the normally-produced carbon dioxide (CO_2). Carbon dioxide (CO_2) is nontoxic and harmless to breathe.

Note that in this last scenario carbon monoxide can be produced even when the appliances are properly adjusted. When the oxygen is 'depleted' or partially used up it means there's not enough to go around. And in the combustion process it takes less oxygen to make CO (with one oxygen atom) than it does to make CO_2 (with two oxygen atoms). So, in a situation with limited oxygen, CO is what gets made.

Carbon monoxide is colorless, odorless, and tasteless. That's what makes it so dangerous. It sneaks up on you.

Hemoglobin is the principle oxygen-carrying compound in your blood. Unfortunately, the attraction or affinity between CO and hemoglobin is many times stronger than the affinity between *oxygen* and hemoglobin so CO displaces the oxygen in your bloodstream. Your brain and heart do not get the oxygen that they need.

Sometimes the first symptom of CO poisoning is simply drowsiness. First you sleep, then you cannot be roused from your sleep, then you die.

Headache is another common symptom of acute carbon monoxide poisoning. (Acute means 'brief and severe.') With oxygen depletion you are pale and confused; with carbon monoxide, you have a headache.

Unfortunately, all kinds of confusion exists surrounding lanterns and carbon monoxide. Truth, half-truth, and outright falsehood are scattered indiscriminately all over the Net.

For example, www.youtube.com/watch?v=EduPzQ0qTyE is a ten-minute video from November 2011 comparing three lanterns: a Petromax (using kerosene as the fuel) and two different Colemans (burning white gas). Camper Al narrates: "You don't want to run a Coleman lantern running white gas in a confined area. Burning white gas tends to generate a significant amount of carbon monoxide . . . not to say kerosene doesn't burn air, but it doesn't produce as much carbon monoxide . . . you don't have nearly the issues with the kerosene lantern as you do with the Coleman lanterns burning white gas."

The more I looked, the more brouhaha I found. I decided it was time to shell out a few bucks for a meter and do my own testing.

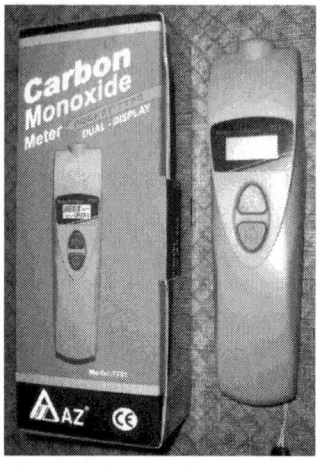

I tested all kinds of lamps and lanterns, one at a time, in a closed room with a CO detector. The detector, factory-preset to 30 ppm (parts per million), never went off. I began to doubt it was even working until I moved a stick of burning incense nearby. Then it *screamed.*

Oops. We need to back up a step and understand parts per million.

One ppm is not very big. A carton of paint at the hardware store holds four one-gallon cans. Visualize, if you will, 17 gallons of paint – a stack of boxes, four high, plus one extra gallon on top. A single drop of paint thinner, measured with an eye-dropper and spread evenly across all 17 gallons, constitutes one part per million.

Okay. Back to the story. Where should I position the detector? Above or below the lamp being tested? It turns out that CO is slightly lighter than air. All other things being equal, CO will not pool in the bathtub. It will spill out over the top of the shower curtain.

It took me a few days to discover the best way to get CO readings. I ended up with lanterns in the bathtub. Atop the shower curtain was a 6" gap between the curtain bar and the shower ceiling. Holding the meter at the gap, just outside the shower (with the shower curtain closed, of course), where the hot/rising gases were spilling out into the bathroom, gave the most consistent readings. Outside the shower, near the ceiling, I could pick up fleeting, transient spikes. At floor level, inside the tub or out, the readings were near zero (after one hour of operation and with the lamp still running). The room itself was 5' x 8' with an 8' ceiling. The meter measured in 1 ppm increments and had a measuring range from zero to 999 ppm. Even in a closed shower stall (with the bathroom door closed), CO proved to be elusive stuff. Out in general living quarters it was virtually impossible to get a reading.

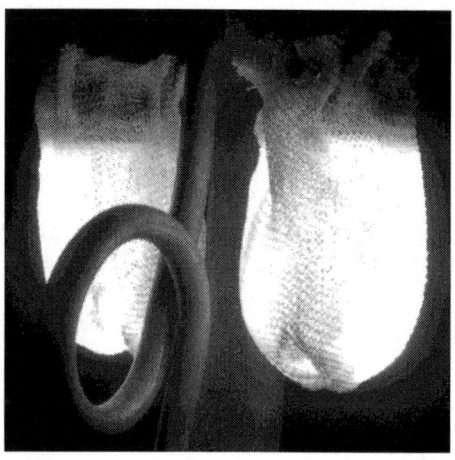

■ **ABOVE:** *Mantles incandesce in the 1600° to 2000° F range. The flame that causes the incandescing must, of necessity, be hotter than that.* ■

My testing contradicted Camper Al. After burning a Coleman 639-with-pricker for one hour inside a closed shower stall with the bathroom door closed, the results were these:

White gas (Coleman fuel) produced an average reading of 10 ppm; a range from 6-to-14 ppm; and transient spikes of 25 ppm.

With the same lantern, kerosene produced an average reading of 16 ppm; a range from 12-to-20 ppm; and transient spikes of 39 ppm.

A Rayo wick-type kerosene lamp (not a pressure lamp and having no mantle) produced an average reading of 20 ppm; a range from 16-to-24 ppm; and transient spikes of 41 ppm.

You can conduct these tests yourself, of course. That's the beauty of the scientific method. You needn't take my word for anything.

The lantern I used, a Coleman 639-with-pricker (not to be confused with the 639C currently being marketed) outputs light on par with a 250-watt light bulb. The 639-with-pricker hails from the 1970's. Unfortunately, it is semi-rare today. Only once or twice a year will you find a 639-with-pricker for sale on eBay. It's the only Coleman I've ever found that will run on white gas AND kerosene AND diesel fuel using today's yttrium mantles. But that makes it perfect for comparison testing.

Terminology

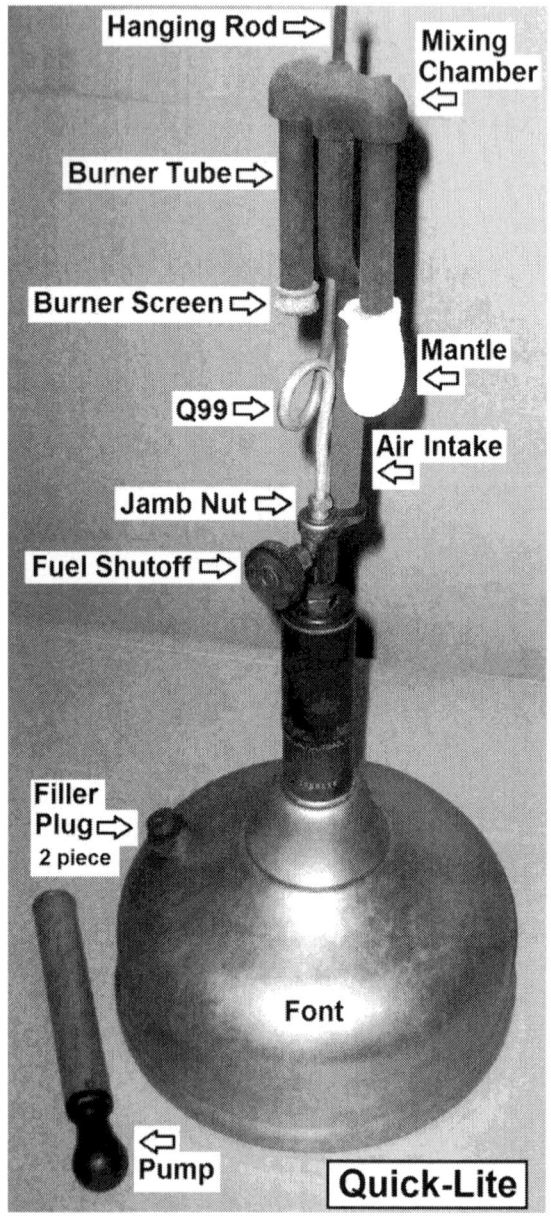

Hanging Rod ⇨

Mixing Chamber ⇦

Burner Tube ⇨

Burner Screen ⇨

Mantle ⇦

Q99 ⇨

Air Intake ⇦

Jamb Nut ⇨

Fuel Shutoff ⇨

Filler Plug ⇨
2 piece

Font

⇦ Pump

Quick-Lite

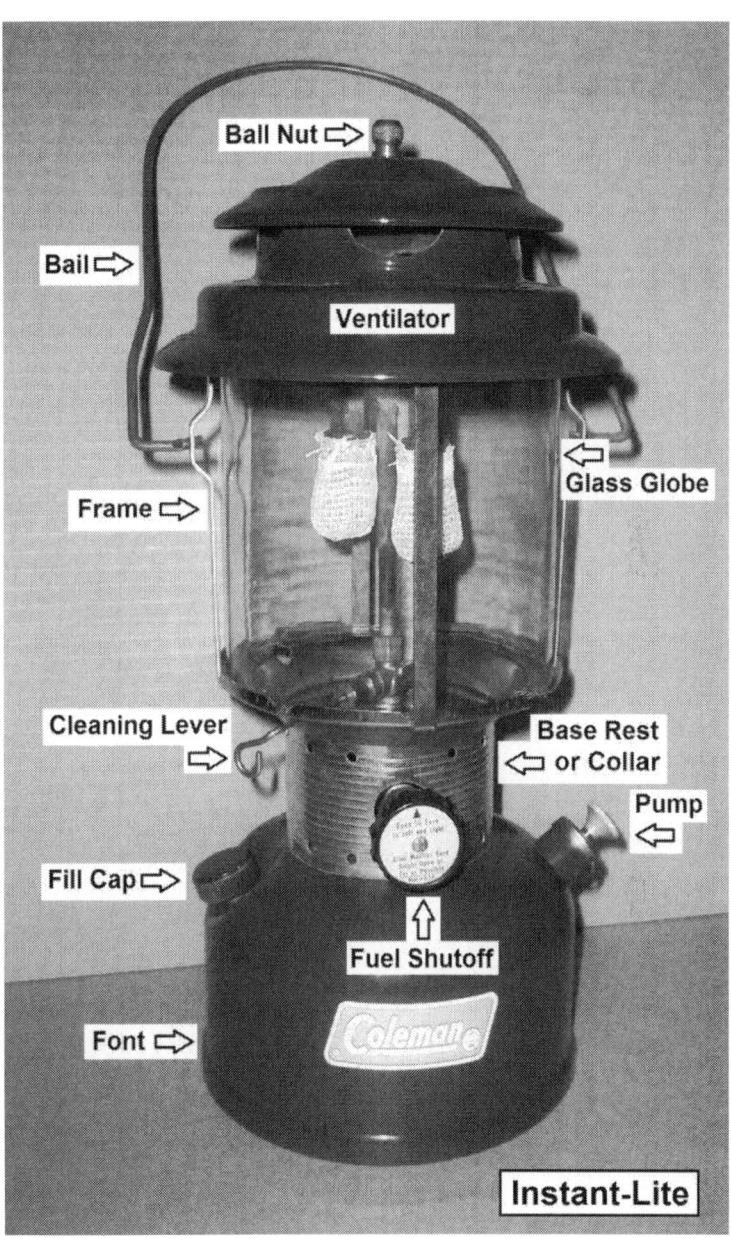

Ball Nut

Bail

Ventilator

Glass Globe

Frame

Cleaning Lever

Base Rest or Collar

Pump

Fill Cap

Fuel Shutoff

Font

Coleman

Instant-Lite

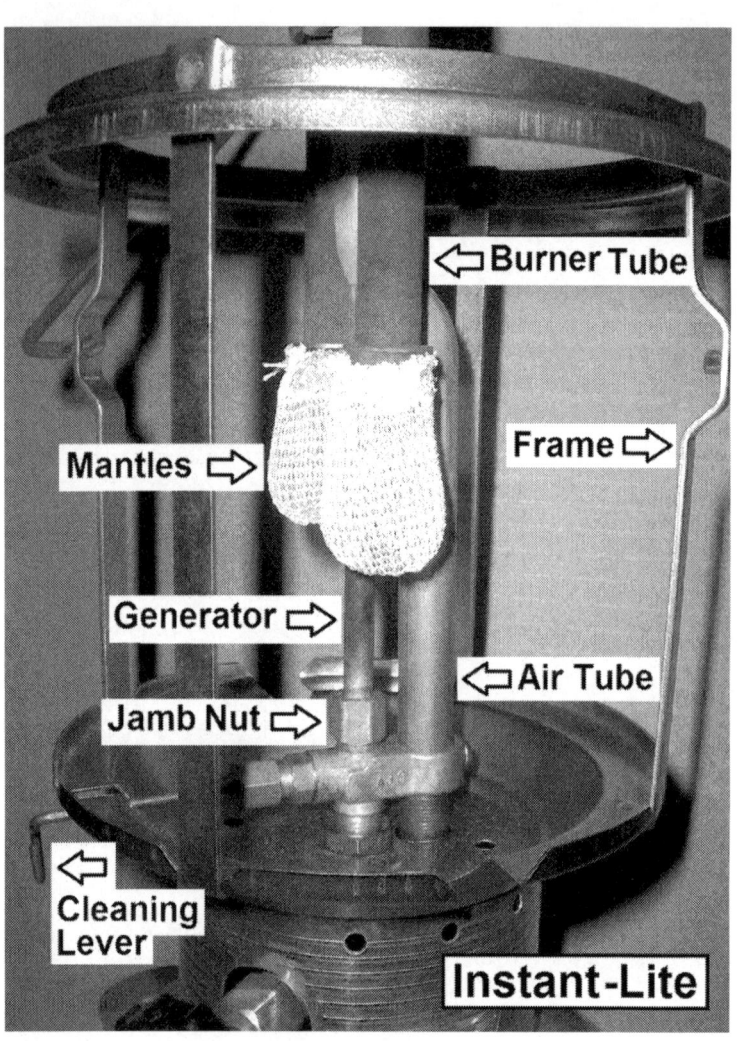

Burner Tube

Frame

Mantles

Generator

Air Tube

Jamb Nut

Cleaning Lever

Instant-Lite

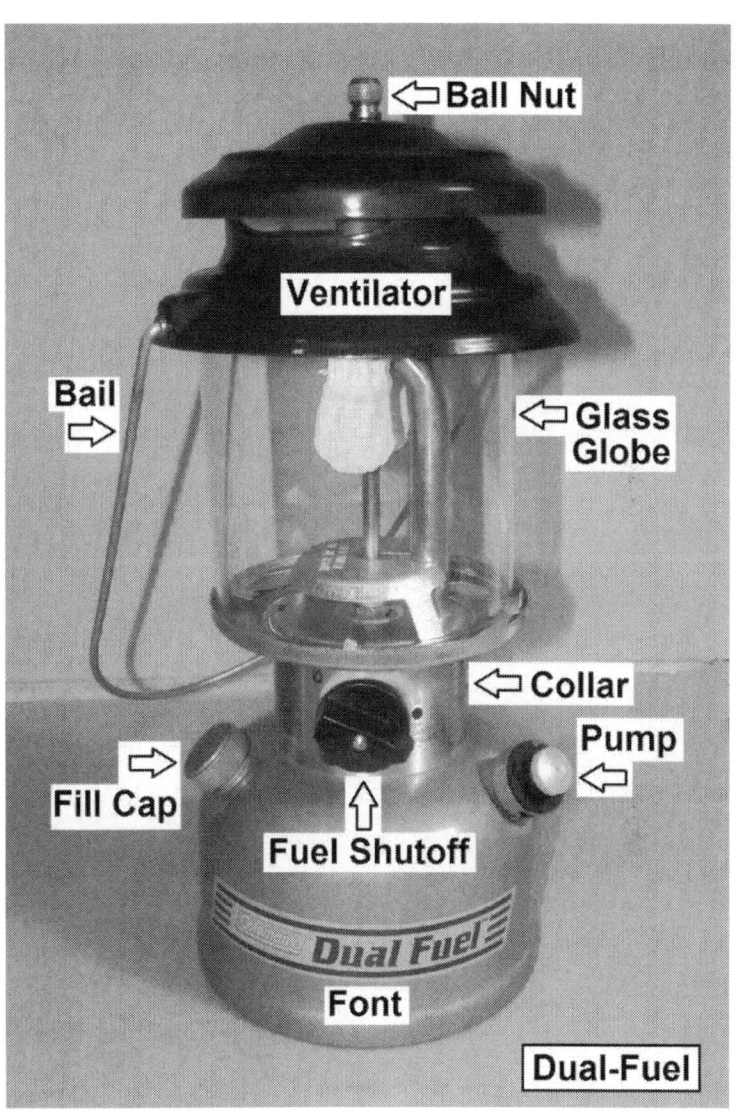

Ball Nut

Ventilator

Bail

Glass Globe

Collar

Pump

Fill Cap

Fuel Shutoff

Font

Dual-Fuel

69

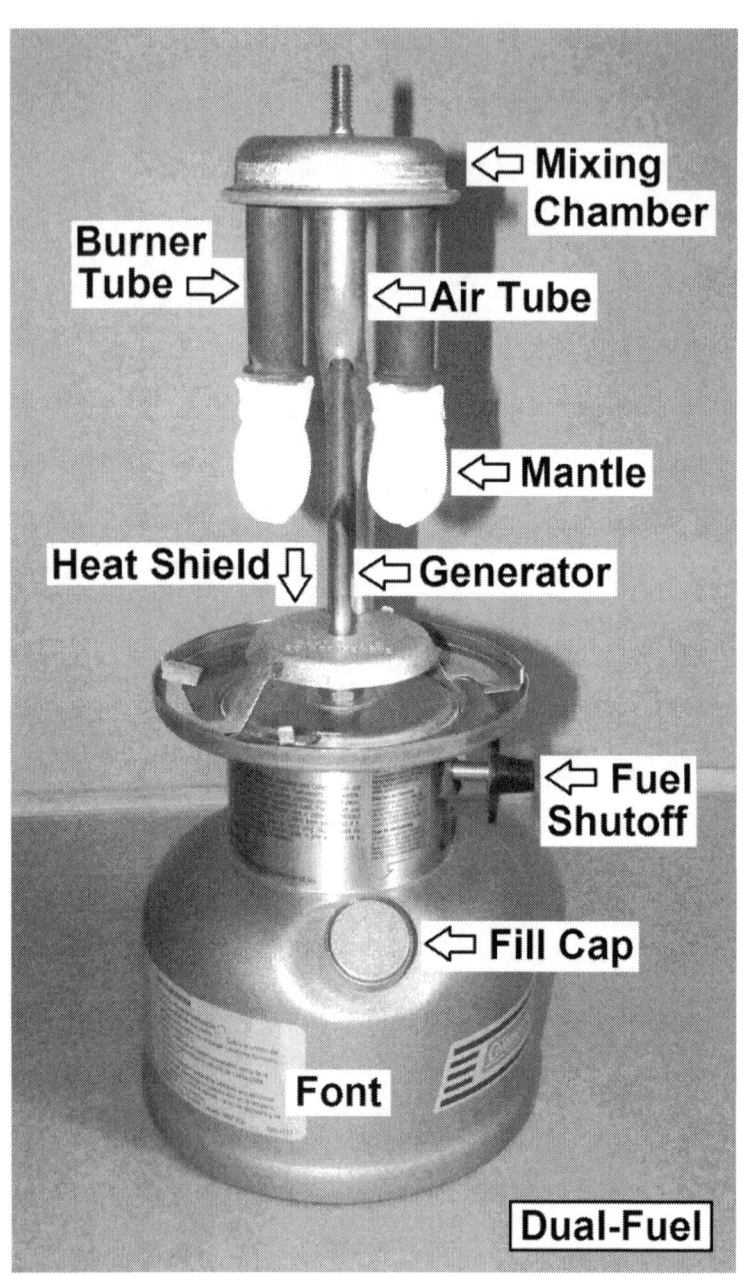

Mixing Chamber

Burner Tube ⇨

⇦ Air Tube

⇦ Mantle

Heat Shield ⇩

⇦ Generator

⇦ Fuel Shutoff

⇦ Fill Cap

Font

Dual-Fuel

70

Printed in Great Britain
by Amazon